Poetry for Young People

Henry Wadsworth Longfellow

Edited by Frances Schoonmaker
Illustrated by Chad Wallace

Sterling Publishing Company, Inc.
New York

To Edgar R. Shannon and his great-great-grandsons, Michael Patrick Bryant and Noah Johnson Dunlap,
"In the round-tower of my heart."

Thanks to Dorothy Lewis for her advice to Sung-Jee Bak for her kind and patient assistance and Theresa Ruyter for
her help with the manuscript.

—Frances

In memory of Michael S. North, Inspiration-Friend
Special thanks to my family, models, and supporters: Mom, Dad, Brett and Scott Wallace; Kate Santino; John, Corinne, Dayna and J.J.
Krachtus; Irene and Jim Pouletsos; Nick, Suzy, Alexandra and Priscilla Thanaside; Kelly Gardiner; Art and Jackie Ryan; Michael and David
Purpura; Todd Macreery; John Thompson; Roger DeMuth; Murray Tinkelman; and the Syracuse University Illustration Dept.

—Chad

Library of Congress Cataloging-in-Publication Data

Longfellow, Henry Wadsworth, 1807-1882.
    Poetry for young people / Henry Wadsworth Longfellow : edited by
Frances Schoonmaker ; illustrated by Chad Wallace.
       p.   cm.
    Includes index.
    Summary: An illustrated selection of twenty-seven complete or
excerpted poems by the renowned nineteenth-century New England poet.
Also includes information about his life.
    ISBN 0-8069-9417-7
    Children's poetry, American. [1. American poetry.]
Schoonmaker, Frances. II. Wallace, Chad, ill. III. Title.
PS2253.S36 1998
811'.3-dc21
                                          98-14833
                                             CIP
                                             AC

3 5 7 9 10 8 6 4 2

Published by Sterling Publishing Company, Inc.
387 Park Avenue South, New York, N.Y. 10016
Introduction © 1998 by Frances Schoonmaker
Illustrations © 1998 by Chad Wallace
Photograph of Henry Wadsworth Longfellow on page 4 courtesy of
Portrait Collection, Rare Books and Manuscript Library, Columbia University
Distributed in Canada by Sterling Publishing
% Canadian Manda Group, One Atlantic Avenue, Suite 105
Toronto, Ontario, Canada M6K 3E7
Distributed in Great Britain and Europe by Cassell PLC
Wellington House, 125 Strand, London WC2R 0BB, England
Distributed in Australia by Capricorn Link (Australia) Pty Ltd.
P.O. Box 6651, Baulkham Hills, Business Centre, NSW 2153, Australia
Printed in Hong Kong
All rights reserved

Sterling ISBN 0-8069-9417-7

Contents

HENRY WADSWORTH LONGFELLOW: "LET US, THEN, BE UP AND DOING"

When Henry Wadsworth Longfellow was born in 1807, Thomas Jefferson was President of the United States. Longfellow's family had been very involved in the American Revolution and in New England life and politics. The Longfellows were respected citizens of Portland, Maine, when skirmishes with the British started. In fact, the home of Henry's great-grand-parents was burned by the British in October of 1775. His grandfather, Stephen, represented their district of Maine in the Massachusetts legislature and was a judge. In those days, Maine was not a separate state. His father, Stephen Longfellow, was a lawyer who had graduat-ed from Harvard. He, too, served in the Massachusetts legislature and was elected to Congress.

Longfellow was named for his mother's brother, Henry Wadsworth, who died heroically in the Navy. Another uncle was a commodore in the Navy. The Wadsworth family was known for outstanding military service. Longfellow's grandfather, General Peleg Wadsworth brought together a company of minutemen and was later put in command of all the troops in eastern Maine during the Revolution. He was captured by the British and imprisoned in a fort. Along with another officer, General Wadsworth made a daring escape from prison. After the war, he, was elected to the Massachusetts legislature and later to Congress.

The Longfellows lived in town in a big, comfortable house that General Wadsworth had built. It was the first brick house in Portland. They had plenty, though they were not a wealthy family. The children took dancing lessons and Longfellow learned to play the piano and flute. His family is said to have had the first piano known in Portland. His parents, Stephen and Zilpah, had a small library and both of them enjoyed literature and encouraged their children to explore the family library and borrow books from the Portland library.

Many of Longfellow's poems are about childhood people and places. Because Portland was a seacoast town, the sea is the subject of many of his poems. In "The Wreck of the Hesperus," on page 21, Longfellow tells a tragic sea story. He wrote in his diary on December 30, 1839, that he had been sitting by the fire until midnight, "when suddenly it came into my mind to write 'The Ballad of the Schooner Hesperus'; which I accordingly did. Then I went to bed, but could not sleep. New thoughts were running in my mind, and I got up to add them to the ballad. It was three by the clock. I then went to bed and fell asleep." Longfellow often worked long into the night writing poetry.

As a boy, he loved to watch the blacksmith at work. He loved the "spreading chestnut tree" under which the blacksmith worked. Years later, in 1879, he tried to save the tree from being chopped down. But Portland city officials wanted to widen the street. Someone suggested that the tree be made into a chair for the poet. Public school children of Cambridge, Massachusetts, where Longfellow lived at the time, gave money for this project. The poet was known to love the company of children and go out of his way to be kind to them. He ordered that any child who wanted to see the chair they had given him should be allowed to do so. Many children came to see the chair — so many that the maids complained about having to wipe their fingerprints off the walls and furniture and their footprints off the floors.

In childhood days, he also watched the potter work at his wheel. To him it seemed to be magic that turned a lump of clay into a pot. In the poem "Turn, Turn," on page 16, Longfellow draws on his memories of the pottery and the mysterious wheel that seemed to sing along with the potter.

When Longfellow was fourteen, he began college. It was not uncommon for young men of his age to go to college. At fifteen, he and his brother, Stephen were allowed to live away from home and attend Bowdoin College in Brunswick. He began to be serious about writing poetry. By his junior year several of his poems had been published. One of his early poems is "Woods in Winter," on page 20. His college room looked out on a pine grove. But it is more likely that the young Longfellow was thinking of Deering's woods, a beautiful grove of oak on the outskirts of Portland. A hawthorn tree stood near the woods and under it was the pottery.

Longfellow's father wanted him to be a lawyer so that he could support himself. But young Henry was determined to be a writer, and a famous one! He wrote to his father, saying that he would be a lawyer in order to "support my *real* existence," as a writer. But something happened to change his father's mind. Longfellow was offered a position as professor in a new field of study at Bowdoin College: modern languages. He was even given money to spend three years in Europe learning the languages! So the eighteen-year-old Henry traveled to Europe to study in France, Spain, Italy, and Germany. He not only prepared himself to teach languages, but he followed his dream of studying literature. He was excited about studying languages. He wrote to one of his sisters, "by every language you learn, a new world is opened before you." Eventually he was able to read, write, and speak French, Italian, Spanish, and German. And he could read Swedish, Finnish, Danish, Norwegian, Dutch, and Portuguese!

When he returned home to begin his work, he married Mary Storer Potter. Mary had grown up in Portland, too. The couple lived in Brunswick for six years. Not only did he continue to write poetry, but he began to be known as an expert on languages. He was offered a position at Harvard as a professor of languages. To prepare for it, he and Mary spent another year in Europe where Longfellow worked to improve his German and studied Scandinavian literature. It was a sad time, however. Mary Longfellow was pregnant and had a miscarriage. She never fully recovered and died within a few weeks. Longfellow threw himself into his work, but he wrote in his diary, "At night I cry myself to sleep like a child."

Longfellow returned to Harvard in the fall of 1836. He taught and wrote for the next eighteen years. Many people of his day thought of him as a scholar and teacher, not as a poet. They used his books on language and literature. But others thought of him as a poet. Today, he is remembered for his poems.

After beginning his work at Harvard, Longfellow found rooms to rent in an old mansion in Cambridge, Massachusetts. It was a house with an interesting history. General Washington had used it as headquarters during the siege of Boston. There were lovely old elm trees in front and a garden behind. Little did he know that one day it would be given to him as a wedding present!

He fell in love with Frances Appleton, a young woman who liked him but did not want to marry him. When he asked her to marry him, "Fanny" turned him down. Longfellow was terribly hurt by this, but continued to be her friend. A few years later, she changed her mind, and they were married in the summer of 1843. His father-in-law, who was quite wealthy, bought the newlyweds the big house where Longfellow had rented rooms. There they were quite happy and entertained many friends in their home. One of their friends was Nathaniel Hawthorne, the famous author. They talked about writing a collection of fairy tales together. And Hawthorne passed along an idea to Longfellow that he used in his most famous poem, "Evangeline." The introduction to "Evangeline" is on page 34. It is a long narrative, or story poem. Hawthorne was very pleased with the poem that Longfellow had written and wrote about it in a New England newspaper. Another friend was Charles Sumner, probably Longfellow's best friend. Sumner was an outspoken abolitionist senator — that is to say, he opposed slavery. He made many enemies, even in the North.

Longfellow was not afraid to have outspoken friends. Nor was he afraid to stand up for what he believed. Once when he was on a ship, returning home from one of his trips abroad, he couldn't sleep. He kept thinking about the Africans who had been stolen from their homes and put in ships to be taken to the United States and sold as slaves. He began to compose a set of eight poems which were published in a little book called *Poems on Slavery*. It took courage to publish them. Longfellow made many enemies by doing so. "The Witnesses," tells about slaves who died when their slave ships were lost at sea (see page 28). "The Slave's Dream" is about a slave who remembers his life in Africa (see page 29). When the Civil War broke out, Longfellow was deeply troubled that the nation had been unable to settle the question of slavery without a war. He wrote the carol, "Christmas Bells," which is on page 31. It is still a popular carol, but two of the verses do not appear with the carol in modern carol books.

For nearly twenty years, the Longfellows were happily settled. They had three daughters and two sons. One of the poems in a famous collection, *Tales of a Wayside Inn,* tells of his affection for his daughters. "The Children's Hour," is on page 40. In this book, Longfellow imagines a group of people meeting at an inn and each telling a story. Each of the stories is interesting to read, but the most famous is "Paul Revere's Ride." On page 43 you can find the first half of the story. This is the part that some people who study Longfellow believe to be the complete part of the poem. The rest was somewhat unfinished and based more on imagination than on facts. So many people have read the poem and loved it that they believe it is the actual history of what happened. But it is actually Longellow's imagination building on a real event.

There are people who think that Longfellow's life was too easy for him to be a real poet. It is true that he lived a comfortable life. But his life was not as easy as it might seem. It took him many years to find his voice as a poet (that is, what he had to say through poetry that would be really unique). And he could not give writing poetry his full attention. He wanted to be a good teacher and continued to write about language and literature. He never got over the death of his first wife and their baby. He knew what it was like to be rejected when Fanny refused to marry him. And, after they had been married for nearly twenty years, she was died in an terrible accident. She was sealing a letter with a candle when her gown caught fire. Longfellow heard her screaming and came running from a nearby room. He grabbed her in his arms and put out the flames, but it was too late. She died from the burns, suffering great pain. Longfellow had serious burns, too. He grieved for her the rest of his life.

He spent his last months by the sea with one of his daughters and her family. He died March 14, 1882. But up until he died, Longfellow kept writing. After he published "A Psalm of Life" (page 36) and a book of poems, *Voices of the Night,* he became a real celebrity. "Hymn to the Night" is also from this book. When *The Song of Hiawatha* was published, people were most eager to read it. It became a favorite. In this poem, Longfellow tells about all of Hiawatha's life. (A section from "Hiawatha's Childhood," is on page 37.) His poetry was just as popular in Europe. People looked for his work, read it, and talked about it. Some of his best loved poems were not his best writing. But people memorized them and used them in their everyday talk about life. As you read his poems, you may notice some lines that seem familiar. That is because people are still using his words in their talk about everyday life, even when they don't know they are quoting Longfellow. Maybe you have heard someone say, "Into each life some rain must fall." This expression comes from "The Rainy Day," on page 12. Or, perhaps you have heard people say they want to leave "footprints on the sands of time." This expression is from "A Psalm of Life," on page 36. Henry Wadsworth Longfellow left many "footprints on the sands of time." They are the poems that we can still enjoy today.

THE ARROW AND THE SONG

I shot an arrow into the air,
It fell to earth, I knew not where;
For, so swiftly it flew, the sight
Could not follow it in its flight.

I breathed a song into the air,
It fell to earth, I knew not where;
For who has sight so keen and strong,
That it can follow the flight of song?

Long, long afterward, in an oak
I found the arrow, still unbroke;
And the song, from beginning to end,
I found again in the heart of a friend.

FOUR BY THE CLOCK

Four by the clock! And yet not day;
But the great world rolls and wheels away,
With its cities on land, and its ships at sea,
Into the dawn that is to be!

Only the lamp in the anchored bark
Sends its glimmer across the dark,
And the heavy breathing of the sea
Is the only sound that comes to me.

bark - *a boat*

DAYBREAK

A wind came up out of the sea,
And said, "O mists, make room for me."

It hailed the ships, and cried, "Sail on,
Ye mariners, the night is gone."

And hurried landward far away,
Crying, "Awake! it is the day."

It said unto the forest, "Shout!
Hang all your leafy banners out!"

It touched the wood-bird's folded wing,
And said, "O bird, awake and sing."

And o'er the farms, "O chanticleer,
Your clarion blow; the day is near."

It whispered to the fields of corn,
"Bow down, and hail the coming morn."

It shouted through the belfry-tower,
"Awake, O bell! proclaim the hour."

It crossed the churchyard with a sigh,
And said, "Not yet! in quiet lie."*

chanticleer——*a rooster*
clarion——*a shrill-sounding trumpet*

Some people believe that all the dead who are buried in graves and churchyards will come to life at the end of time.

THE RAINY DAY

The day is cold, and dark, and dreary;
It rains, and the wind is never weary;
The vine still clings to the mouldering wall,
But at every gust the dead leaves fall,
And the day is dark and dreary.

My life is cold, and dark, and dreary;
It rains, and the wind is never weary;
My thoughts still cling to the mouldering Past,
But the hopes of youth fall thick in the blast,
And the days are dark and dreary.

Be still, sad heart! And cease repining;
Behind the clouds is the sun still shining;
Thy fate is the common fate of all,
Into each life some rain must fall,
Some days must be dark and dreary.

mouldering—*moldy or overgrown with mold*
repining—*feeling unhappy or discontented*

THE VILLAGE BLACKSMITH

Under a spreading chestnut-tree
 The village smithy stands;
The smith, a mighty man is he,
 With large and sinewy hands;
And the muscles of his brawny arms
 Are strong as iron bands.

His hair is crisp, and black, and long,
 His face is like the tan;
His brow is wet with honest sweat,
 He earns whate'er he can,
And looks the whole world in the face,
 For he owes not any man.

Week in, week out, from morn till night,
 You can hear his bellows blow;
You can hear him swing his heavy sledge,
 With measured beat and slow,
Like a sexton ringing the village bell,
 When the evening sun is low.

And children coming home from school
 Look in at the open door;
They love to see the flaming forge,
 And hear the bellows roar,
And catch the burning sparks that fly
 Like chaff from a threshing-floor.

He goes on Sunday to the church,
 And sits among his boys;
He hears the parson pray and preach,
 He hears his daughter's voice,
Singing in the village choir,
 And it makes his heart rejoice.

It sounds to him like her mother's voice,
    Singing in Paradise!
He needs must think of her once more
    How in the grave she lies;
And with his hard, rough hand he wipes
    A tear out of his eyes.

Toiling,—rejoicing,—sorrowing,
    Onward through life he goes;
Each morning sees some task begin,
    Each evening sees it close;
Something attempted, something done,
    Has earned a night's repose.

Thanks, thanks to thee, my worthy friend,
    For the lesson thou hast taught!
Thus at the flaming forge of life
    Our fortunes must be wrought;
Thus on its sounding anvil shaped
    Each burning deed and thought.

sinewy— *strong, tough*

bellows—*A tool the blacksmith uses to pump air on a fire to make it hotter.*

sexton— *One who rings the church bells. Sometimes the sexton is the one who helps care for the church.*

chaff—*the husks that grow on grain that are separated by threshing*

anvil—*the smith uses an anvil, or block of iron, to put his work on when he is shaping it*

TURN, TURN, MY WHEEL*

*Turn, turn, my wheel! Turn round and round
Without a pause, without a sound:
    So spins the flying world away!
This clay, well mixed with marl and sand,
Follows the motion of my hand;
For some must follow, and some command,
    Though all are made of clay!*

Thus sang the Potter at his task
Beneath the blossoming hawthorn-tree,
While o'er his features, like a mask,
The quilted sunshine and leaf-shade
Moved, as the boughs above him swayed,
And clothed him, till he seemed to be
A figure woven in tapestry,
So sumptuously was he arrayed
In that magnificent attire
Of sable tissue flaked with fire.
Like a magician he appeared,
A conjurer without book or beard;
And while he plied his magic art—
For it was magical to me—
I stood in silence and apart,
And wondered more and more to see
That shapeless, lifeless mass of clay
Rise up to meet the master's hand,
And now contract and now expand,
And even his slightest touch obey.

*"Turn, Turn, My Wheel" is from a much longer poem, "Keramos."

marl—*a red-colored clay soil*
sumptuously—*costly and magnificently decorated*

16

AFTERMATH

When the summer fields are mown,
When the birds are fledged and flown,
    And the dry leaves strew the path;
With the falling of the snow,
With the cawing of the crow,
Once again the fields we mow
    And gather in the aftermath.

Not the sweet, new grass with flowers
Is this harvesting of ours;
    Not the upland clover bloom;
But the rowen mixed with weeds,
Tangled tufts from marsh and meads,
Where the poppy drops its seeds
    In the silence and the gloom.

fledged—*a young bird that is grown with all its feathers*
rowen—*the second growth of a crop of hay or grass during the growing season; it is*
    also known as aftermath, the title Longfellow chose for the poem.
meads—*meadows, fields*

HAUNTED HOUSES*

All houses wherein men have lived and died
    Are haunted houses. Through the open doors
The harmless phantoms on their errands glide,
    With feet that make no sound upon the floors.

We meet them at the doorway, on the stair,
    Along the passages they come and go,
Impalpable impressions on the air,
    A sense of something moving to and fro.

There are more guests at the table than the hosts
    Invited; the illuminated hall
Is thronged with quiet, inoffensive ghosts,
    As silent as the pictures on the wall.

The stranger at my fireside cannot see
    The forms I see, nor hear the sounds I hear;
He but perceives what is; while unto me
    All that has been is visible and clear.

*These are the beginning stanzas of a longer poem in which
Longfellow thinks about how our lives are connected to those
who have lived and died before us.

WOODS IN WINTER

When winter winds are piercing chill,
    And through the hawthorn blows the gale,
With solemn feet I tread the hill,
    That overbrows the lonely vale.

O'er the bare upland, and away
    Through the long reach of desert woods,
The embracing sunbeams chastely play,
    And gladden these deep solitudes.

Where, twisted round the barren oak,
    The summer vine in beauty clung,
And summer winds the stillness broke,
    The crystal icicle is hung.

Where, from their frozen urns, mute springs
    Pour out the river's gradual tide,
Shrilly the skater's iron rings,
    And voices fill the wooden side.

Alas! How changed from the fair scene,
    When birds sang out their mellow lay,
And winds were soft, and woods were green,
    And the song ceased not with the day!

But still wild music is abroad,
    Pale, desert woods! within your crowd;
And gathering winds, in hoarse accord,
    Amid the vocal reeds pipe loud.

Chill airs and wintry winds! my ear
    Has grown familiar with your song;
I hear it in the opening year,
    I listen, and it cheers me long.

chastely—*innocently, purely*

THE WRECK OF THE HESPERUS

It was the schooner Hesperus,
    That sailed the wintry sea;
And skipper had taken his little daughter,
    To bear him company.

Blue were her eyes as the fairy-flax,
    Her cheeks like the dawn of day,
And her bosom white as the hawthorn buds,
    That ope in the month of May.

The skipper he stood beside the helm,
    His pipe was in his mouth,
And he watched how the veering flaw did blow
    The smoke now West, now South.

Then up and spake an old Sailor,
    Had sailed to the Spanish Main,
"I pray thee, put into yonder port,
    For I fear a hurricane.

"Last night, the moon had a golden ring,
    And to-night no moon we see!"
The skipper, he blew a whiff from his pipe,
    And a scornful laugh laughed he.

Colder and louder blew the wind,
    A gale from the Northeast,
The snow fell hissing in the brine,
    And the billows frothed like yeast.

Down came the storm, and smote amain
    The vessel in its strength;
She shuddered and paused, like a frightened steed,
    Then leaped her cable's length.

"Come hither! Come hither! My little daughter,
    And do not tremble so;
For I can weather the roughest gale
    That ever wind did blow."

He wrapped her warm in his seaman's coat
    And against the stinging blast;
He cut a rope from a broken spar,
    And bound her to the mast.

"O father! I hear the church-bells ring,
    Oh say, what may it be?"
"'T is a fog-bell on a rock-bound coast!"—
    And he steered for the open sea.

"O father! I hear the sound of guns,
    Oh say, what may it be?"
"Some ship in distress, that cannot live
    In such an angry sea!"

"O father! I see a gleaming light,
    Oh say, what may it be?"
But the father answered never a word,
    A frozen corpse was he.

Lashed to the helm, all stiff and stark,
    With his face turned to the skies,
The lantern gleamed through the gleaming snow
    On his fixed and glassy eyes.

Then the maiden clasped her hands and prayed
    That saved she might be;
And she thought of Christ, who stilled the wave,
    On the Lake of Galilee.

And fast through the midnight dark and drear,
    Through the whistling sleet and snow,
Like a sheeted ghost, the vessel swept
    Tow'rds the reef of Norman's Woe.

And ever the fitful gusts between
    A sound came from the land;
It was the sound of the trampling surf
    On the rocks and the hard sea-sand.

The breakers were right beneath her bows,
    She drifted a dreary wreck,
And a whooping billow swept the crew
    Like icicles from her deck.

She struck where the white and fleecy waves
    Looked soft as carded wool,
But the cruel rocks, they gored her side
    Like the horns of an angry bull.

Her rattling shrouds, all sheathed in ice,
    With the masts went by the board;
Like a vessel of glass, she strove and sank,
    Ho! Ho! The breakers roared!

At daybreak on the bleak sea-beach,
    A fisherman stood aghast,
To see the form of a maiden fair,
    Lashed close to a drifting mast.

The salt sea was frozen on her breast,
    The salt tears in her eyes;
And he saw her hair, like the brown sea-weed,
    On the billows fall and rise.

Such was the wreck of the Hesperus,
    In the midnight and the snow!
Christ save us all from a death like this,
    On the reef of Norman's Woe!

ope—*open*
flaw—*a sudden gust of wind, often with rain or snow*
amain—*forcefully, and at great speed*
carded wool—*wool fiber that has been combed into thread
   with a wire brush*

THE SOUND OF THE SEA

The sea awoke at midnight from its sleep,
    And round the pebbly beaches far and wide
    I heard the first wave of the rising tide
Rush onward with uninterrupted sweep;

A voice out of the silence of the deep,
    A sound mysteriously multiplied
    As of a cataract from the mountain's side,
Or roar of winds upon a wooded steep.

So comes to us at times, from the unknown
    And inaccessible solitudes of being,
    The rushing of the sea-tides of the soul;

And inspirations, that we deem our own,
    Are some divine foreshadowing and foreseeing
    Of things beyond our reason or control.

cataract—*waterfall*

BECALMED

Becalmed upon the sea of Thought,
Still unattained the land it sought,
My mind, with loosely-hanging sails,
Lies waiting the auspicious gales.

On either side, behind, before,
The ocean stretches like a floor,—
A level floor of amethyst,
Crowned by a golden dome of mist.

Blow, breath of inspiration, blow!
Shake and uplift this golden glow!
And fill the canvas of the mind
With wafts of thy celestial wind.

Blow, breath of song! until I feel
The straining sail, the lifting keel,
The life of the awakening sea,
Its motion and its mystery!

auspicious—*favorable*
amethyst—*a precious stone of blue-violet or purple*
celestial—*heavenly*

THE TIDE RISES, THE TIDE FALLS

The tide rises, the tide falls,
The twilight darkens, the curlew calls;
Along the sea-sands damp and brown
The traveller hastens toward the town,
  And the tide rises, the tide falls.

Darkness settles on roofs and walls,
But the sea, the sea in the darkness calls;
The little waves, with their soft, white hands,
Efface the footprints in the sands,
  And the tide rises, the tide falls.

The morning breaks; the steeds in their stalls
Stamp and neigh, as the hostler calls;
The day returns, but nevermore
Returns the traveller to the shore,
  And the tide rises, the tide falls.

curlew—*a large brown wading bird with long legs*
hostler—*stableman; groom*

THE WITNESSES

In Ocean's wide domains,
    Half buried in the sands,
Lie skeletons in chains,
    With shackled feet and hands.

Beyond the fall of dews,
    Deeper than plummet lies,
Float ships, with all their crews,
    No more to sink nor rise.

There the black Slave-ship swims,
    Freighted with human forms,
Whose fettered, fleshless limbs
    Are not the sport of storms.

These are the bones of Slaves;
    They gleam from the abyss;
They cry, from yawning waves,
    "We are the Witnesses!"

Within Earth's wide domains
    Are markets for men's lives;
Their necks are galled with chains,
    Their wrists are cramped with gyves.

Dead bodies, that the kite
    In deserts makes its prey;
Murders, that with affright
    Scare school-boys from their play!

All evil thoughts and deeds;
    Anger, and lust, and pride;
The foulest, rankest weeds,
    That choke Life's groaning tide!

These are the woes of Slaves;
    They glare from the abyss;
They cry, from unknown graves,
    "We are the Witnesses!"

gyves—*shackles*
plummet—*a heavy weight used by builders to keep walls*
    in a straight line. It also means to weigh down, like a
    dead weight.
fettered—*chained;shackled*
galled—*sore and irritated*
kite—*bird of prey like the*
    hawk or falcon

THE SLAVE'S DREAM

Beside the ungathered rice he lay,
    His sickle in his hand;
His breast was bare, his matted hair
    Was buried in the sand.
Again, in the mist and shadow of sleep,
    He saw his Native land.

Wide through the landscape of his dreams
    The lordly Niger flowed;
Beneath the palm-trees on the plain
    Once more a king he strode;
And heard the tinkling caravans
    Descend the mountain road.

He saw once more his dark-eyed queen
    Among her children stand;
They clasped his neck, they kissed his cheeks,
    They held him by the hand!—
A tear burst from the sleeper's lids
    And fell into the sand.

And then at furious speed he rode
    Along the Niger's bank;
His bridle-reins were golden chains,
    And, with a martial clank,
At each leap he could feel his scabbard of steel
    Smiting his stallion's flank.

Before him, like a blood-red flag,
    The bright flamingoes flew;
From morn till night he followed their flight,
    O'er plains where the tamarind grew,
Till he saw the roofs of Caffre huts,
    And the ocean rose to view.

At night he heard the lion roar,
    And the hyena scream,

And the river-horse, as he crushed the reeds
    Beside some hidden stream;
And it passed, like a glorious roll of drums,
    Through the triumph of his dream.

The forests with their myriad tongues,
    Shouted of liberty;
And the Blast of the Desert cried aloud,
    With a voice so wild and free,
That he started in his sleep and smiled
    At their tempestuous glee.

He did not feel the driver's whip,
    Nor the burning heat of day;
For Death had illumined the Land of Sleep,
    And his lifeless body lay
A worn-out fetter, that the soul
    Had broken and thrown away!

Niger—a river in Africa
scabbard—the case that protects the blade of a
    sword
tamarind—a tropical tree with yellow flowers
Caffre—a South African from the Bantu people
river-horse—the hippopotamus
myriad—a countless number of things

FRAGMENTS

December 18, 1847

Soft through the silent air descend the feathery snow-flakes;
White are the distant hills, white are the neighboring fields;
Only the marshes are brown, and the river rolling among them
Weareth the leaden hue seen in the eyes of the blind.

SNOW-FLAKES

Out of the bosom of the air,
        Out of the cloud-folds of her garments shaken,
Over the woodlands brown and bare,
        Over the harvest-fields forsaken,
Silent, and soft, and slow
Descends the snow.

Even as our cloudy fancies take
        Suddenly shape in some divine expression,
Even as the troubled heart doth make
        In the white countenance confession,
The troubled sky reveals
The grief it feels.

This is the poem of the air,
        Slowly in silent syllables recorded;
This the secret of despair,
        Long in its cloudy bosom hoarded,
Now whispered and revealed
To wood and field.

countenance—*appearance, expression on the face*

30

CHRISTMAS BELLS*

I heard the bells on Christmas Day
Their old, familiar carols play,
And wild and sweet
The words repeat
Of peace on earth, good-will to men!

And thought how, as the day had come,
The belfries of all Christendom
Had rolled along
The unbroken song
Of peace on earth, good-will to men!

Till, ringing, singing on its way,
The world revolved from night to day,
A voice, a chime,
A chant sublime
Of peace on earth, good-will to men!

Then from each black, accursed mouth
The cannon thundered in the South,
And with the sound
The carols drowned
Of peace on earth, good-will to men!

It was as if an earthquake rent
The hearth-stones of a continent,
And made forlorn
The households born
Of peace on earth, good-will to men!

And in despair I bowed my head;
"There is no peace on earth," I said;
"For hate is strong,
And mocks the song
Of peace on earth, good-will to men!"

Then pealed the bells more loud and deep:
"God is not dead; nor doth he sleep!
The Wrong shall fail,
The Right prevail,
With peace on earth, good-will to men!"

*The Civil War in the United States took place between 1861 and 1865. This poem was written in 1864.

31

AFTERNOON IN FEBRUARY

The day is ending,
The night is descending;
The marsh is frozen,
The river dead.

Through clouds like ashes
The red sun flashes
On village windows
That glimmer red.

The snow recommences;
The buried fences
Mark no longer
The road o'er the plain;

While through the meadows
Like fearful shadows,
Slowly passes
A funeral train.

The bell is pealing,
And every feeling
Within me responds
To the dismal knell;

Shadows are trailing,
My heart is bewailing
And tolling within
Like a funeral bell.

32

HAROUN AL RASCHID

One day, Haroun Al Raschid read
A book wherein the poet said:—

"Where are the kings, and where the rest
Of those who once the world possessed?

"They're gone with all their pomp and show,
They're gone the way that thou shalt go.

"O thou who choosest for thy share
The world, and what the world calls fair,

"Take all that it can give or lend,
But know that death is at the end!"

Haroun Al Raschid bowed his head:
Tears fell upon the page he read.

THE FOREST PRIMEVAL*

This is the forest primeval. The murmuring pines and the hemlocks,
Bearded with moss, and in garments green, indistinct in the twilight,
Stand like Druids of eld, with voices sad and prophetic,
Stand like harpers hoar, with beards that rest on their bosoms.
Loud from its rocky caverns, the deep-voiced neighboring ocean
Speaks, and in accents disconsolate answers the wail of the forest.

This is the introduction to the long narrative (story) poem, "Evangeline."

eld—*old*

harpers hoar—*hoar means greyish-white; here Longfellow probably intends it to
mean hoar hair, or gray hair to go with the harper's long beard. The harper is a
person who plays a harp.*

A PSALM OF LIFE

Tell me not, in mournful numbers,
    Life is but an empty dream!—
For the soul is dead that slumbers,
    And things are not what they seem.

Life is real! Life is earnest!
    And the grave is not its goal;
Dust thou art, to dust returnest,
    Was not spoken of the soul.

Not enjoyment, and not sorrow,
    Is our destined end or way;
But to act, that each to-morrow
    Find us farther than to-day.

Art is long, and Time is fleeting,
    And our hearts, though stout and brave,
Still, like muffled drums, are beating
    Funeral marches to the grave.

In the world's broad field of battle,
    In the bivouac of Life,
Be not like dumb, driven cattle!
    Be a hero in the strife!

Trust no Future, howe'er pleasant!
    Let the dead Past bury its dead!
Act,—act in the living Present!
    Heart within, and God o'erhead!

Lives of great men all remind us
    We can make our lives sublime,
And, departing, leave behind us
    Footprints on the sands of time;

Footprints, that perhaps another,
    Sailing o'er life's solemn main,
A forlorn and shipwrecked brother,
    Seeing, shall take heart again.

Let us, then, be up and doing,
    With a heart for any fate;
Still achieving, still pursuing,
    Learn to labor and to wait.

bivouac—*a soldier's temporary camp*

HIAWATHA'S CHILDHOOD*

By the shores of Gitche Gumee,
By the shining Big-Sea-Water,
Stood the wigwam of Nokomis,
daughter of the Moon, Nokomis.
Dark behind it rose the forest,
Rose the black and gloomy pine-trees,
Rose the firs with cones upon them;
Bright before it beat the water,
Beat the clear and sunny water,
Beat the shining Big-Sea-Water.

There the wrinkled old Nokomis
Nursed the little Hiawatha,
Rocked him in his linden cradle,
Bedded soft in moss and rushes,
Safely bound with reindeer sinews;
Stilled his fretful wail by saying,
"Hush! the Naked Bear will hear thee!"
Lulled him into slumber, singing,
"Ewa-yea! my little owlet!
Who is this, that lights the wigwam?
With his great eyes lights the wigwam?
Ewa-yea! my little owlet!"

Many things Nokomis taught him
Of the stars that shine in heaven;
Showed him Ishkoodah, the comet,
Ishkoodah, with fiery tresses;
Showed the Death-Dance of the spirits,
Warriors with their plumes and war-clubs,
Flying far away to northward
In the frosty nights of Winter;
Showed the broad white road in heaven,
Pathway of the ghosts, the shadows,
Running straight across the heavens,
Crowded with the ghosts, the shadows.

At the door on summer evenings
Sat the little Hiawatha;
Heard the whispering of the pine-trees,
Heard the lapping of the waters,
Sounds of music, words of wonder;
"Minne-wawa!" said the pine-trees,
"Mudway-aushka!" said the water.

Saw the fire-fly, Wah-wah-taysee,
Flitting through the dusk of evening,
With the twinkle of its candle
Lighting up the brakes and bushes,
And he sang the song of children,
Sang the song Nokomis taught him:
"Wah-wah-taysee, little fire-fly,
Little, flitting, white-fire insect,
Little, dancing, white-fire creature,
Light me with your little candle,
Ere upon my bed I lay me,
Ere in sleep I close my eyelids!"
Saw the moon rise from the water
Rippling, rounding from the water,
Saw the flecks and shadows on it,
Whispered, "What is that Nokomis?"
And the good Nokomis answered:
"Once a warrior, very angry,
Seized his grandmother and threw her
Up into the sky at midnight;
Right against the moon he threw her;
'T is her body that you see there."

Saw the rainbow in the heaven,
In the eastern sky, the rainbow
Whispered, "What is that, Nokomis?"
And the good Nokomis answered:
"'T is the heaven of flowers you see there
All the wild-flowers of the forest,
All the lilies of the prairie,
When on earth they fade and perish,
Blossom in that heaven above us."

When he heard the owls at midnight,
Hooting, laughing in the forest,
"What is that?" he cried in terror,
"What is that," he said, "Nokomis?"
And the good Nokomis answered:
"That is but the owl and owlet,
Talking in their native language,
Talking, scolding at each other."

Then the little Hiawatha
Learned of every bird its language,
Learned their names and all their secrets,
How they built their nests in Summer,
Where they hid themselves in Winter,
Talked with them when'er he met them,
Called them "Hiawatha's Chickens."

Of all the beasts he learned the language,
Learned their names and all their secrets,
How the beavers built their lodges,
Where the squirrels hid their acorns,
How the reindeer ran so swiftly,
Why the rabbit was so timid,
Talked with them whene'er he met them,
Called them "Hiawatha's Brothers."

*This poem has been taken from a much longer work
called "The Song of Hiawatha."

linden—*a family of trees with great heart shaped leaves
and flexible branches*
broad white road in heaven—*the Milky Way*

39

THE CHILDREN'S HOUR

Between the dark and the daylight,
    When the night is beginning to lower,
Comes a pause in the day's occupations,
    That is known as the Children's Hour.

I hear in the chamber above me
    The patter of little feet,
The sound of a door that is opened,
    And voices soft and sweet.

From my study I see in the lamplight,
    Descending the broad hall stair,
Grave Alice, and laughing Allegra,
    And Edith with golden hair.

A whisper, and then a silence:
    Yet I know by their merry eyes
They are plotting and planning together
    To take me by surprise.

A sudden rush from the stairway,
    A sudden raid from the hall!
By three doors left unguarded
    They enter my castle wall!

They climb up into my turret
    O'er the arms and back of my chair;
If I try to escape, they surround me;
    They seem to be everywhere.

They almost devour me with kisses,
    Their arms about me entwine,
Till I think of the Bishop of Bingen
    In his Mouse-Tower on the Rhine!

Do you think, O blue-eyed banditti,
    Because you have scaled the wall,
Such an old mustache as I am
    Is not a match for you all!

I have you fast in my fortress,
    And will not let you depart,
But put you down into the dungeon,
    In the round-tower of my heart.

And there will I keep you forever,
    Yes, forever and a day,
Till the walls shall crumble to ruin,
    And moulder in dust away!

banditti—*bandits or robbers*

PAUL REVERE'S RIDE*

Listen, my children, and you shall hear
Of the midnight ride of Paul Revere,
On the eighteenth of April, in Seventy-five;
Hardly a man is now alive
Who remembers that famous day and year.

He said to his friend, "If the British march
By land or sea from the town to-night,
Hang a lantern aloft in the belfry arch
Of the North Church tower as a signal light,—
One if by land, and two, if by sea;
And I on the opposite shore will be,
Ready to ride and spread the alarm
Through every Middlesex village and farm,
For the country folk to be up and to arm."

Then he said, "Good-night!" and with muffled oar
Silently rowed to the Charlestown shore,
Just as the moon rose over the bay,
Where swinging wide at her moorings lay
The Somerset, British man-of-war;
A phantom ship, with each mast and spar
Across the moon like a prison bar,
And a huge black hulk, that was magnified
By its own reflection in the tide.

Meanwhile, his friend, through alley and street,
Wanders and watches with eager ears,
Till in the silence around him he hears
The muster of men at the barrack door,
The sound of arms, and the tramp of feet,
And the measured tread of the grenadiers,
Marching down to their boats on the shore.

Then he climbed the tower of the Old North Church,
By the wooden stairs, with stealthy tread,
To the belfry-chamber overhead,

43

And startled the pigeons from their perch
On the sombre rafters, that round him made
Masses and moving shapes of shade,—
By the trembling ladder, steep and tall,
To the highest window in the wall,
Where he paused to listen and look down
A moment on the roofs of the town,
And the moonlight flowing over all.

Beneath, in the churchyard, lay the dead,
In their night-encampment on the hill,
Wrapped in silence so deep and still
That he could hear, like a sentinel's tread,
The watchful night-wind, as it went
Creeping along from tent to tent,
And seeming to whisper, "All is well!"
A moment only he feels the spell
Of the place and the hour, and the secret dread
Of the lonely belfry and the dead;
For suddenly all his thoughts are bent
On a shadowy something far away,
Where the river widens to meet the bay,—
A line of black that bends and floats
On the rising tide, like a bridge of boats.

Meanwhile, impatient to mount and ride,
Booted and spurred, with a heavy stride
On the opposite shore walked Paul Revere.,
Now he patted his horse's side,
Now gazed at the landscape far and near,
Then, impetuous, stamped the earth,
And turned and tightened his saddle-girth;
But mostly he watched with eager search
The belfry-tower of the Old North Church,
As it rose above the graves on the hill,
Lonely and spectral and sombre and still.
And lo! As he looks, on the belfry's height
A glimmer, and then a gleam of light!
He springs to the saddle, the bridle he turns,

But lingers and gazes, till full on his sight
A second lamp in the belfry burns!

A hurry of hoofs in a village street,
A shape in the moonlight, a bulk in the dark,
And beneath, from the pebbles, in passing, a spark
Struck out by a steed flying fearless
      and fleet;
That was all! And yet, through the
      gloom and the light,
The fate of a nation was riding
      that night.

*This is the first part of the poem "Paul Revere's Ride."

grenadiers—*infantry or foot soldiers*
impetuous—*forcefully*
spectral—*ghost like*

HYMN TO THE NIGHT

I heard the trailing garments of the Night
    Sweep through her marble halls!
I saw her sable skirts all fringed with light
    From the celestial walls!

I felt her presence, by its spell of might,
    Stoop o'er me from above;
The calm, majestic presence of the Night,
    As of the one I love.

I heard the sounds of sorrow and delight,
    The manifold, soft chimes,
That fill the haunted chambers of the Night,
    Like some old poet's rhymes.

From the cool cisterns of the midnight air
    My spirit drank repose;
The fountain of perpetual peace flows there,—
    From those deep cisterns flows.

O holy Night! From thee I learn to bear
    What man has borne before!
Thou layest thy finger on the lips of Care,
    And they complain no more.

Peace! Peace! Orestes-like I breathe this prayer!
    Descend with broad-winged flight,
The welcome, the thrice-prayed for, the most fair,
    The best-beloved Night!

Orestes—*a character in a Greek myth who, with his sister Electra, avenged the death of his father.*
manifold—*something that has many forms*
cisterns—*tanks that hold water*

CURFEW

I

Solemnly, mournfully,
    Dealing its dole,
The Curfew Bell
    Is beginning to toll.

Cover the embers,
    And put out the light;
Toil comes with the morning,
    And rest with the night.

Dark grow the windows,
    And quenched is the fire;
Sound fades into silence,—
    All footsteps retire.

No voice in the chambers,
    No sound in the hall!
Sleep and oblivion
    Reign over all!

II

The book is completed,
    And closed, like the day;
And the hand that has written it
    Lays it away.

Dim grow its fancies;
    Forgotten they lie;
Like coals in the ashes,
    They darken and die.

Song sinks into silence,
    The story is told,
The windows are darkened,
    The hearth-stone is cold.

Darker and darker
    The black shadows fall;
Sleep and oblivion
    Reign over all.

dole—*to give something out in small bits.*
oblivion—*forgetting, forgetfulness*

Index